This reading journal belongs to:

....

"Today a reader, tomorrow a leader."

– Margaret Fuller

How to use this reading logbook journal:

This journal has enough space for 104 books, if you read 1 book per week it's great for 2 years, or if you read 1 book every two weeks it's good for 4 years.

There is a table of content with page numbers, so you can easily look up any book in the journal.

At the end of the journal, you will find additional pages for notes, a list of books you want to read next, a list for books you have borrowed and another one for books you lent out.

There are 2 pages for every book with prompts to be completed in the first part. And enough space to write down notes, ideas and takeaways about the books you read.

When taking notes and takeaways from a book, consider the following questions: What did you learn? What insights did you gain? Does the book make a unique contribution to knowledge or wisdom? Does it provide a new and better way to present difficult material? What surprised you? Did you ever have an ah-ha moment while reading the book? What is your favorite quote from the book? **Why?** (you can write down your favourite quote or the best takeaway on the bottom left corner on the sticky note). **How can you describe the book in one sentence? What creative value does this book contribute? Would you recommend this book to others, and why?**

Tony Robbins has said that the **quality of your life is determined by the quality of the questions you ask,** so make sure you ask the right questions!

BOOKSHELF

BOOKSHELF

Book & Author	Page
	60
	62
	64
	66
	68
	70
	72
	74
	76
	78
	80
	82
	84
	86
	88
	90
	92
	94
	96
	98
	100
	102
	104
	106
	108
	110

BOOKSHELF

Book & Author	Page
	112
	114
	116
	118
	120
	122
	124
	126
	128
	130
	132
	134
	136
	138
	140
	142
	144
	146
	148
	150
	152
	154
	156
	158
	160
	162

BOOKSHELF

Book & Author	Page
	164
	166
	168
	170
	172
	174
	176
	178
	180
	182
	184
	186
	188
	190
	192
	194
	196
	198
	200
	202
	204
	206
	208
	210
	212
	214

Book title:

Author:

Date started:	Date finished:	No of pages:	My rating: ☆☆☆☆☆

○ Fiction
Genre:

○ Non-fiction
Subject:

Format:
○ 📕 ○ 📱 ○ 🎧

I've read the book:
In-full ○   Partially ○   Skimming ○

Thoughts / Notes / Ideas

Additional Notes / Comments / Takeaways / Quotes

Book title:

Author:

Date started:

Date finished:

No of pages:

My rating:
☆ ☆ ☆ ☆ ☆

◯ Fiction
Genre:

◯ Non-fiction
Subject:

Format:
◯ 📕 ◯ 📱 ◯ 🎧

I've read the book:
In-full   Partially   Skimming
◯   ◯   ◯

Thoughts / Notes / Ideas

Additional Notes / Comments / Takeaways / Quotes

Book title:

Author:

Date started:	Date finished:	No of pages:	My rating:
			☆ ☆ ☆ ☆ ☆

○ Fiction
Genre:

○ Non-fiction
Subject:

Format:
○ 📕 ○ 📄 ○ 🎧

I've read the book:
In-full   Partially   Skimming
  ○   ○   ○

Thoughts / Notes / Ideas

Additional Notes / Comments / Takeaways / Quotes

Book title:

Author:

Date started:	Date finished:	No of pages:	My rating:
			☆ ☆ ☆ ☆ ☆

○ Fiction
Genre:

○ Non-fiction
Subject:

Format:
○ 📕   ○ 📱   ○ 🎧

I've read the book:
In-full ○   Partially ○   Skimming ○

Thoughts / Notes / Ideas

Additional Notes / Comments / Takeaways / Quotes

Book title:

Author:

Date started:	Date finished:	No of pages:	My rating:
			☆ ☆ ☆ ☆ ☆

◯ Fiction
Genre:

◯ Non-fiction
Subject:

Format:
◯ 📕 ◯ 📱 ◯ 🎧

I've read the book:

In-full	Partially	Skimming
◯	◯	◯

Thoughts / Notes / Ideas

Additional Notes / Comments / Takeaways / Quotes

Book title:

Author:

Date started:	Date finished:	No of pages:	My rating:
			☆ ☆ ☆ ☆ ☆

○ Fiction
Genre:
○ Non-fiction
Subject:

Format:
○ 📕 ○ 📱 ○ 🎧

I've read the book:
In-full ○   Partially ○   Skimming ○

Thoughts / Notes / Ideas

Additional Notes / Comments / Takeaways / Quotes

Book title:

Author:

| Date started: | Date finished: | No of pages: | My rating: ☆ ☆ ☆ ☆ ☆ |

○ Fiction
Genre:

○ Non-fiction
Subject:

Format:
○ 📕 ○ 📱 ○ 🎧

I've read the book:
In-full   Partially   Skimming
○   ○   ○

Thoughts / Notes / Ideas

Additional Notes / Comments / Takeaways / Quotes

Book title:

Author:

Date started: | Date finished: | No of pages: | My rating:
☆ ☆ ☆ ☆ ☆

○ Fiction
Genre:

○ Non-fiction
Subject:

Format:
○ ○ ○

I've read the book:
In-full ○ Partially ○ Skimming ○

Thoughts / Notes / Ideas

Additional Notes / Comments / Takeaways / Quotes

Book title:

Author:

Date started:

Date finished:

No of pages:

My rating:
☆ ☆ ☆ ☆ ☆

○ Fiction
  Genre:

○ Non-fiction
  Subject:

Format:
○ 📕 ○ 📱 ○ 🎧

I've read the book:
In-full   Partially   Skimming
○   ○   ○

Thoughts / Notes / Ideas

Book title:

Author:

Date started:	Date finished:	No of pages:	My rating:
			☆ ☆ ☆ ☆ ☆

○ Fiction
Genre:

○ Non-fiction
Subject:

Format:
○ 📕 ○ 📱 ○ 🎧

I've read the book:
In-full   Partially   Skimming
○   ○   ○

Thoughts / Notes / Ideas

Additional Notes / Comments / Takeaways / Quotes

Book title:

Author:

Date started:

Date finished:

No of pages:

My rating:
☆ ☆ ☆ ☆ ☆

○ Fiction
  Genre:

○ Non-fiction
  Subject:

Format:
○ 📕 ○ 📱 ○ 🎧

I've read the book:
In-full   Partially   Skimming
   ○   ○   ○

Thoughts / Notes / Ideas

Additional Notes / Comments / Takeaways / Quotes

Book title:

Author:

Date started:

Date finished:

No of pages:

My rating:
☆ ☆ ☆ ☆ ☆

○ Fiction
Genre:

○ Non-fiction
Subject:

Format:

I've read the book:

In-full   Partially   Skimming
○   ○   ○

Thoughts / Notes / Ideas

Additional Notes / Comments / Takeaways / Quotes

Book title:

Author:

Date started:	Date finished:	No of pages:	My rating:
			☆ ☆ ☆ ☆ ☆

○ Fiction
Genre:

○ Non-fiction
Subject:

Format:
○ 📕 ○ 📱 ○ 🎧

I've read the book:
In-full Partially Skimming
○   ○   ○

Thoughts / Notes / Ideas

Additional Notes / Comments / Takeaways / Quotes

Book title:

Author:

Date started:

Date finished:

No of pages:

My rating:
☆ ☆ ☆ ☆ ☆

○ Fiction
Genre:

○ Non-fiction
Subject:

Format:
○ ■ ○ 📱 ○ 🎧

I've read the book:
In-full   Partially   Skimming
○   ○   ○

Thoughts / Notes / Ideas

Additional Notes / Comments / Takeaways / Quotes

Book title:

Author:

Date started:

Date finished:

No of pages:

My rating:
☆ ☆ ☆ ☆ ☆

○ Fiction
Genre:

○ Non-fiction
Subject:

Format:
○ 📕 ○ 📱 ○ 🎧

I've read the book:
In-full   Partially   Skimming
○   ○   ○

Thoughts / Notes / Ideas

Additional Notes / Comments / Takeaways / Quotes

Book title:

Author:

Date started: | Date finished: | No of pages: | My rating:
☆ ☆ ☆ ☆ ☆

○ Fiction
Genre:
○ Non-fiction
Subject:

Format:
○ 📕 ○ 📱 ○ 🎧

I've read the book:
In-full   Partially   Skimming
○   ○   ○

Thoughts / Notes / Ideas

Additional Notes / Comments / Takeaways / Quotes

Book title:

Author:

| Date started: | Date finished: | No of pages: | My rating: ☆ ☆ ☆ ☆ ☆ |

○ Fiction   ○ Non-fiction
  Genre: Subject:

Format: ○ 📕 ○ 📄 ○ 🎧

I've read the book:
In-full ○   Partially ○   Skimming ○

Thoughts / Notes / Ideas

Additional Notes / Comments / Takeaways / Quotes

Book title:

Author:

Date started: | **Date finished:** | **No of pages:** | **My rating:**
☆ ☆ ☆ ☆ ☆

◯ Fiction
   Genre:

◯ Non-fiction
   Subject:

Format:
◯ 📕 ◯ 📱 ◯ 🎧

I've read the book:
In-full   Partially   Skimming
◯   ◯   ◯

Thoughts / Notes / Ideas

Additional Notes / Comments / Takeaways / Quotes

Book title:

Author:

Date started:	Date finished:	No of pages:	My rating:
			☆ ☆ ☆ ☆ ☆

○ Fiction
Genre:

○ Non-fiction
Subject:

Format:
○ 📕 ○ 📱 ○ 🎧

I've read the book:

In-full   Partially   Skimming
○   ○   ○

Thoughts / Notes / Ideas

Additional Notes / Comments / Takeaways / Quotes

Book title:

Author:

Date started:

Date finished:

No of pages:

My rating:
☆ ☆ ☆ ☆ ☆

○ Fiction
Genre:

○ Non-fiction
Subject:

Format:
○ 📕 ○ 📱 ○ 🎧

I've read the book:
In-full   Partially   Skimming
○   ○   ○

Thoughts / Notes / Ideas

Additional Notes / Comments / Takeaways / Quotes

Book title:

Author:

Date started:

Date finished:

No of pages:

My rating:
☆ ☆ ☆ ☆ ☆

○ Fiction
Genre:

○ Non-fiction
Subject:

Format:
○ 📕 ○ 📱 ○ 🎧

I've read the book:

In-full ○   Partially ○   Skimming ○

Thoughts / Notes / Ideas

Additional Notes / Comments / Takeaways / Quotes

Book title:

Author:

Date started: Date finished: No of pages: My rating:
☆☆☆☆☆

○ Fiction
   Genre:

○ Non-fiction
   Subject:

Format:
○ 📖   ○ 📱   ○ 🎧

I've read the book:
In-full   Partially   Skimming
○   ○   ○

Thoughts / Notes / Ideas

Additional Notes / Comments / Takeaways / Quotes

Book title:

Author:

Date started: | Date finished: | No of pages: | My rating:
☆ ☆ ☆ ☆ ☆

○ Fiction
Genre:

○ Non-fiction
Subject:

Format:
○ 📕 ○ 📱 ○ 🎧

I've read the book:
In-full Partially Skimming
○   ○   ○

Thoughts / Notes / Ideas

Additional Notes / Comments / Takeaways / Quotes

Book title:

Author:

Date started:	Date finished:	No of pages:	My rating: ☆☆☆☆☆

○ Fiction
Genre:

○ Non-fiction
Subject:

Format:
○ 📖 ○ 📱 ○ 🎧

I've read the book:
In-full ○   Partially ○   Skimming ○

Thoughts / Notes / Ideas

Additional Notes / Comments / Takeaways / Quotes

Book title:

Author:

Date started: | Date finished: | No of pages: | My rating:
☆ ☆ ☆ ☆ ☆

○ Fiction
Genre:
○ Non-fiction
Subject:

Format:
○ 📖 ○ 📱 ○ 🎧

I've read the book:
In-full ○   Partially ○   Skimming ○

Thoughts / Notes / Ideas

Additional Notes / Comments / Takeaways / Quotes

Book title:

Author:

Date started:

Date finished:

No of pages:

My rating:
☆ ☆ ☆ ☆ ☆

◯ Fiction
Genre:

◯ Non-fiction
Subject:

Format:
◯ 📕 ◯ 📱 ◯ 🎧

I've read the book:

In-full ◯　　Partially ◯　　Skimming ◯

Thoughts / Notes / Ideas

Additional Notes / Comments / Takeaways / Quotes

Book title:

Author:

Date started:

Date finished:

No of pages:

My rating:
☆ ☆ ☆ ☆ ☆

○ Fiction
Genre:

○ Non-fiction
Subject:

Format:
○ 📖 ○ 📱 ○ 🎧

I've read the book:

In-full ○   Partially ○   Skimming ○

Thoughts / Notes / Ideas

Additional Notes / Comments / Takeaways / Quotes

Book title:

Author:

Date started:	Date finished:	No of pages:	My rating:
			☆ ☆ ☆ ☆ ☆

○ Fiction
  Genre:

○ Non-fiction
  Subject:

Format:
○ 📖 ○ 📱 ○ 🎧

I've read the book:
In-full   Partially   Skimming
  ○   ○   ○

Thoughts / Notes / Ideas

Additional Notes / Comments / Takeaways / Quotes

Book title:

Author:

Date started:	Date finished:	No of pages:	My rating:
			☆ ☆ ☆ ☆ ☆

○ Fiction
　Genre:

○ Non-fiction
　Subject:

Format:
○ 📕　○ 📱　○ 🎧

I've read the book:
In-full　　Partially　　Skimming
○　　　　　○　　　　　○

Thoughts / Notes / Ideas

Additional Notes / Comments / Takeaways / Quotes

Book title:

Author:

Date started:	Date finished:	No of pages:	My rating:
			☆ ☆ ☆ ☆ ☆

○ Fiction
Genre:

○ Non-fiction
Subject:

Format:
○ 📖 ○ 📄 ○ 🎧

I've read the book:

In-full ○   Partially ○   Skimming ○

Thoughts / Notes / Ideas

Additional Notes / Comments / Takeaways / Quotes

Book title:

Author:

Date started:

Date finished:

No of pages:

My rating:
☆ ☆ ☆ ☆ ☆

○ Fiction
Genre:

○ Non-fiction
Subject:

Format:

I've read the book:

In-full ○   Partially ○   Skimming ○

Thoughts / Notes / Ideas

Additional Notes / Comments / Takeaways / Quotes

Book title:

Author:

Date started: | Date finished: | No of pages: | My rating:
☆ ☆ ☆ ☆ ☆

◯ Fiction   ◯ Non-fiction
Genre: Subject:

Format:

I've read the book:
In-full   Partially   Skimming
◯   ◯   ◯

Thoughts / Notes / Ideas

Additional Notes / Comments / Takeaways / Quotes

Book title:

Author:

Date started: | Date finished: | No of pages: | My rating:
☆ ☆ ☆ ☆ ☆

○ Fiction
   Genre:

○ Non-fiction
   Subject:

Format:
○ 📕 ○ 📱 ○ 🎧

I've read the book:
In-full ○   Partially ○   Skimming ○

Thoughts / Notes / Ideas

Additional Notes / Comments / Takeaways / Quotes

Book title:

Author:

Date started:

Date finished:

No of pages:

My rating:
☆ ☆ ☆ ☆ ☆

◯ Fiction
Genre:

◯ Non-fiction
Subject:

Format:

I've read the book:

In-full ◯   Partially ◯   Skimming ◯

Thoughts / Notes / Ideas

Additional Notes / Comments / Takeaways / Quotes

Book title:

Author:

Date started:

Date finished:

No of pages:

My rating:
☆ ☆ ☆ ☆ ☆

○ Fiction
Genre:

○ Non-fiction
Subject:

Format:
○ 📕 ○ 📱 ○ 🎧

I've read the book:
In-full   Partially   Skimming
○   ○   ○

Thoughts / Notes / Ideas

Additional Notes / Comments / Takeaways / Quotes

Book title:

Author:

Date started:	Date finished:	No of pages:	My rating:
			☆ ☆ ☆ ☆ ☆

○ Fiction
Genre:

○ Non-fiction
Subject:

Format:
○ 📕 ○ 📄 ○ 🎧

I've read the book:
In-full ○   Partially ○   Skimming ○

Thoughts / Notes / Ideas

Additional Notes / Comments / Takeaways / Quotes

Book title:

Author:

Date started:	Date finished:	No of pages:	My rating:
			☆ ☆ ☆ ☆ ☆

○ Fiction
   Genre:

○ Non-fiction
   Subject:

Format:
○ 📕 ○ 📱 ○ 🎧

I've read the book:
In-full   Partially   Skimming
  ○   ○   ○

Thoughts / Notes / Ideas

Additional Notes / Comments / Takeaways / Quotes

Book title:

Author:

Date started:

Date finished:

No of pages:

My rating:
☆ ☆ ☆ ☆ ☆

◯ Fiction
Genre:

◯ Non-fiction
Subject:

Format:

I've read the book:

In-full ◯   Partially ◯   Skimming ◯

Thoughts / Notes / Ideas

Additional Notes / Comments / Takeaways / Quotes

Book title:

Author:

Date started: | Date finished: | No of pages: | My rating:
☆ ☆ ☆ ☆ ☆

◯ Fiction ◯ Non-fiction
Genre: Subject:

Format:
◯ 📕 ◯ 📱 ◯ 🎧

I've read the book:
In-full Partially Skimming
◯ ◯ ◯

Thoughts / Notes / Ideas

Additional Notes / Comments / Takeaways / Quotes

Book title:

Author:

Date started:

Date finished:

No of pages:

My rating:
☆ ☆ ☆ ☆ ☆

○ Fiction   ○ Non-fiction
Genre: Subject:

Format:
○ 📖 ○ 📱 ○ 🎧

I've read the book:
In-full   Partially   Skimming
○   ○   ○

Thoughts / Notes / Ideas

Additional Notes / Comments / Takeaways / Quotes

Book title:

Author:

Date started: | Date finished: | No of pages: | My rating:
☆☆☆☆☆

○ Fiction
  Genre:

○ Non-fiction
  Subject:

Format:
○ 📕 ○ 📱 ○ 🎧

I've read the book:
In-full   Partially   Skimming
○   ○   ○

Thoughts / Notes / Ideas

Additional Notes / Comments / Takeaways / Quotes

Book title:

Author:

Date started:	Date finished:	No of pages:	My rating:
			☆ ☆ ☆ ☆ ☆

○ Fiction
Genre:

○ Non-fiction
Subject:

Format:
○ ○ ○

I've read the book:
In-full   Partially   Skimming
○   ○   ○

Thoughts / Notes / Ideas

Additional Notes / Comments / Takeaways / Quotes

Book title:

Author:

Date started:	Date finished:	No of pages:	My rating:
			☆ ☆ ☆ ☆ ☆

○ Fiction   ○ Non-fiction
  Genre: Subject:

Format:
○ 📕 ○ 📱 ○ 🎧

I've read the book:
In-full   Partially   Skimming
○   ○   ○

Thoughts / Notes / Ideas

Additional Notes / Comments / Takeaways / Quotes

Book title:

Author:

Date started:	Date finished:	No of pages:	My rating:
			☆ ☆ ☆ ☆ ☆

○ Fiction   ○ Non-fiction
  Genre: Subject:

Format:
○ 📕   ○ 📱   ○ 🎧

I've read the book:
In-full   Partially   Skimming
○   ○   ○

Thoughts / Notes / Ideas

Additional Notes / Comments / Takeaways / Quotes

Book title:

Author:

Date started:	Date finished:	No of pages:	My rating:
			☆ ☆ ☆ ☆ ☆

○ Fiction
 Genre:

○ Non-fiction
 Subject:

Format:
○ 📘 ○ 📱 ○ 🎧

I've read the book:

In-full	Partially	Skimming
○	○	○

Thoughts / Notes / Ideas

Additional Notes / Comments / Takeaways / Quotes

Book title:

Author:

Date started:	Date finished:	No of pages:	My rating:
			☆ ☆ ☆ ☆ ☆

○ Fiction
Genre:

○ Non-fiction
Subject:

Format:
○ 📖 ○ 📱 ○ 🎧

I've read the book:
In-full ○   Partially ○   Skimming ○

Thoughts / Notes / Ideas

Additional Notes / Comments / Takeaways / Quotes

Book title:

Author:

Date started:	Date finished:	No of pages:	My rating:
			☆ ☆ ☆ ☆ ☆

○ Fiction
Genre:

○ Non-fiction
Subject:

Format:
○ 📖 ○ 📱 ○ 🎧

I've read the book:
In-full ○   Partially ○   Skimming ○

Thoughts / Notes / Ideas

Additional Notes / Comments / Takeaways / Quotes

Book title:

Author:

Date started:

Date finished:

No of pages:

My rating:
☆ ☆ ☆ ☆ ☆

○ Fiction
   Genre:

○ Non-fiction
   Subject:

Format:
○ 📕   ○ 📱   ○ 🎧

I've read the book:

In-full	Partially	Skimming
○	○	○

Thoughts / Notes / Ideas

Additional Notes / Comments / Takeaways / Quotes

Book title:

Author:

Date started: | **Date finished:** | **No of pages:** | **My rating:**
☆ ☆ ☆ ☆ ☆

○ Fiction
Genre:

○ Non-fiction
Subject:

Format:
○ ○ ○

I've read the book:
In-full   Partially   Skimming
○   ○   ○

Thoughts / Notes / Ideas

Additional Notes / Comments / Takeaways / Quotes

Book title:

Author:

Date started:	Date finished:	No of pages:	My rating:
			☆ ☆ ☆ ☆ ☆

○ Fiction
Genre:

○ Non-fiction
Subject:

Format:
○ 📕 ○ 📱 ○ 🎧

I've read the book:
In-full ○   Partially ○   Skimming ○

Thoughts / Notes / Ideas

Additional Notes / Comments / Takeaways / Quotes

Book title:

Author:

Date started:	Date finished:	No of pages:	My rating:
			☆ ☆ ☆ ☆ ☆

○ Fiction
  Genre:

○ Non-fiction
  Subject:

Format:
○ 📕 ○ 📱 ○ 🎧

I've read the book:
In-full ○   Partially ○   Skimming ○

Thoughts / Notes / Ideas

Additional Notes / Comments / Takeaways / Quotes

Book title:

Author:

Date started:	Date finished:	No of pages:	My rating:
			☆ ☆ ☆ ☆ ☆

◯ Fiction
Genre:

◯ Non-fiction
Subject:

Format:
◯ 📕 ◯ 📱 ◯ 🎧

I've read the book:

In-full   Partially   Skimming
◯   ◯   ◯

Thoughts / Notes / Ideas

Additional Notes / Comments / Takeaways / Quotes

Book title:

Author:

Date started:

Date finished:

No of pages:

My rating:
☆ ☆ ☆ ☆ ☆

○ Fiction
Genre:

○ Non-fiction
Subject:

Format:
○ ▮ ○ ▤ ○ 🎧

I've read the book:
In-full   Partially   Skimming
○   ○   ○

Thoughts / Notes / Ideas

Additional Notes / Comments / Takeaways / Quotes

Book title:

Author:

Date started:	Date finished:	No of pages:	My rating:
			☆ ☆ ☆ ☆ ☆

○ Fiction
Genre:

○ Non-fiction
Subject:

Format:
○ 📕 ○ 📱 ○ 🎧

I've read the book:
In-full ○   Partially ○   Skimming ○

Thoughts / Notes / Ideas

Additional Notes / Comments / Takeaways / Quotes

Book title:

Author:

| Date started: | Date finished: | No of pages: | My rating: ☆ ☆ ☆ ☆ ☆ |

○ Fiction
Genre:
○ Non-fiction
Subject:

Format:

I've read the book:
In-full ○ Partially ○ Skimming ○

Thoughts / Notes / Ideas

Additional Notes / Comments / Takeaways / Quotes

Book title:

Author:

Date started:

Date finished:

No of pages:

My rating:
☆ ☆ ☆ ☆ ☆

○ Fiction
Genre:

○ Non-fiction
Subject:

Format:
○ ▓ ○ ▤ ○ 🎧

I've read the book:
In-full   Partially   Skimming
○   ○   ○

Thoughts / Notes / Ideas

Additional Notes / Comments / Takeaways / Quotes

Book title:

Author:

Date started:	Date finished:	No of pages:	My rating:
			☆ ☆ ☆ ☆ ☆

○ Fiction
Genre:

○ Non-fiction
Subject:

Format:
○ 📕 ○ 📱 ○ 🎧

I've read the book:
In-full ○   Partially ○   Skimming ○

Thoughts / Notes / Ideas

Book title:

Author:

Date started:

Date finished:

No of pages:

My rating:
☆ ☆ ☆ ☆ ☆

○ Fiction
Genre:

○ Non-fiction
Subject:

Format:
○ 📕 ○ 📱 ○ 🎧

I've read the book:
In-full   Partially   Skimming
○   ○   ○

Thoughts / Notes / Ideas

Additional Notes / Comments / Takeaways / Quotes

Book title:

Author:

Date started:	Date finished:	No of pages:	My rating:
			☆ ☆ ☆ ☆ ☆

○ Fiction   ○ Non-fiction
Genre: Subject:

Format:
○ 📘   ○ 📱   ○ 🎧

I've read the book:
In-full   Partially   Skimming
○   ○   ○

Thoughts / Notes / Ideas

Additional Notes / Comments / Takeaways / Quotes

Book title:

Author:

Date started:	Date finished:	No of pages:	My rating:
			☆ ☆ ☆ ☆ ☆

○ Fiction
Genre:

○ Non-fiction
Subject:

Format:
○ 📕 ○ 📱 ○ 🎧

I've read the book:
In-full ○   Partially ○   Skimming ○

Thoughts / Notes / Ideas

Additional Notes / Comments / Takeaways / Quotes

Book title:

Author:

Date started:

Date finished:

No of pages:

My rating:
☆ ☆ ☆ ☆ ☆

◯ Fiction
Genre:

◯ Non-fiction
Subject:

Format:

I've read the book:
In-full   Partially   Skimming
◯   ◯   ◯

Thoughts / Notes / Ideas

Additional Notes / Comments / Takeaways / Quotes

Book title:

Author:

Date started:	Date finished:	No of pages:	My rating:
			☆ ☆ ☆ ☆ ☆

○ Fiction ○ Non-fiction
Genre: Subject:

Format:
○ 📕 ○ 📱 ○ 🎧

I've read the book:
In-full   Partially   Skimming
○   ○   ○

Thoughts / Notes / Ideas

Additional Notes / Comments / Takeaways / Quotes

Book title:

Author:

Date started:

Date finished:

No of pages:

My rating:
☆ ☆ ☆ ☆ ☆

○ Fiction
Genre:

○ Non-fiction
Subject:

Format:
○ ○ ○

I've read the book:
In-full   Partially   Skimming
○   ○   ○

Thoughts / Notes / Ideas

Additional Notes / Comments / Takeaways / Quotes

Book title:

Author:

Date started:

Date finished:

No of pages:

My rating:
☆ ☆ ☆ ☆ ☆

◯ Fiction
Genre:

◯ Non-fiction
Subject:

Format:
◯ ◯ ◯

I've read the book:
In-full   Partially   Skimming
◯   ◯   ◯

Thoughts / Notes / Ideas

Additional Notes / Comments / Takeaways / Quotes

Book title:

Author:

Date started:

Date finished:

No of pages:

My rating:
☆ ☆ ☆ ☆ ☆

○ Fiction
　Genre:

○ Non-fiction
　Subject:

Format:

I've read the book:

In-full　　Partially　　Skimming
○　　　　　○　　　　　○

Thoughts / Notes / Ideas

Additional Notes / Comments / Takeaways / Quotes

Book title:

Author:

Date started:	Date finished:	No of pages:	My rating:
			☆ ☆ ☆ ☆ ☆

○ Fiction　　○ Non-fiction
　Genre:　　　　Subject:

Format:
○ 📕　○ 📱　○ 🎧

I've read the book:
In-full　　Partially　　Skimming
　○　　　　　○　　　　　　○

Thoughts / Notes / Ideas

Additional Notes / Comments / Takeaways / Quotes

Book title:

Author:

Date started:

Date finished:

No of pages:

My rating:
☆ ☆ ☆ ☆ ☆

○ Fiction
Genre:

○ Non-fiction
Subject:

Format:
○ ○ ○

I've read the book:
In-full Partially Skimming
○   ○   ○

Thoughts / Notes / Ideas

Additional Notes / Comments / Takeaways / Quotes

Book title:

Author:

Date started:

Date finished:

No of pages:

My rating:
☆ ☆ ☆ ☆ ☆

○ Fiction
Genre:

○ Non-fiction
Subject:

Format:
○ 📕 ○ 📱 ○ 🎧

I've read the book:
In-full   Partially   Skimming
○   ○   ○

Thoughts / Notes / Ideas

Additional Notes / Comments / Takeaways / Quotes

Book title:

Author:

| Date started: | Date finished: | No of pages: | My rating: ☆ ☆ ☆ ☆ ☆ |

○ Fiction
Genre:

○ Non-fiction
Subject:

Format: ○ ▮ ○ ▤ ○ 🎧

I've read the book:

In-full ○   Partially ○   Skimming ○

Thoughts / Notes / Ideas

Additional Notes / Comments / Takeaways / Quotes

Book title:

Author:

Date started:	Date finished:	No of pages:	My rating:
			☆ ☆ ☆ ☆ ☆

○ Fiction
Genre:

○ Non-fiction
Subject:

Format:
○ 📔 ○ 📖 ○ 🎧

I've read the book:
In-full   Partially   Skimming
○   ○   ○

Thoughts / Notes / Ideas

Additional Notes / Comments / Takeaways / Quotes

Book title:

Author:

Date started:

Date finished:

No of pages:

My rating:
☆ ☆ ☆ ☆ ☆

◯ Fiction
Genre:

◯ Non-fiction
Subject:

Format:
◯ 📕 ◯ 📱 ◯ 🎧

I've read the book:
In-full   Partially   Skimming
◯   ◯   ◯

Thoughts / Notes / Ideas

Additional Notes / Comments / Takeaways / Quotes

Book title:

Author:

Date started:	Date finished:	No of pages:	My rating:
			☆ ☆ ☆ ☆ ☆

○ Fiction
Genre:

○ Non-fiction
Subject:

Format:
○ 📕 ○ 📱 ○ 🎧

I've read the book:
In-full   Partially   Skimming
○   ○   ○

Thoughts / Notes / Ideas

Additional Notes / Comments / Takeaways / Quotes

Book title:

Author:

Date started:	Date finished:	No of pages:	My rating:
			☆ ☆ ☆ ☆ ☆

○ Fiction
  Genre:

○ Non-fiction
  Subject:

Format:
○ ▪ ○ ▥ ○ 🎧

I've read the book:
In-full   Partially   Skimming
  ○   ○   ○

Thoughts / Notes / Ideas

Additional Notes / Comments / Takeaways / Quotes

Book title:

Author:

Date started:	Date finished:	No of pages:	My rating: ☆ ☆ ☆ ☆ ☆

○ Fiction
Genre:

○ Non-fiction
Subject:

Format: ○ 📕 ○ 📱 ○ 🎧

I've read the book:
In-full ○   Partially ○   Skimming ○

Thoughts / Notes / Ideas

Additional Notes / Comments / Takeaways / Quotes

Book title:

Author:

| Date started: | Date finished: | No of pages: | My rating: ☆☆☆☆☆ |

◯ Fiction Genre: ◯ Non-fiction Subject:

Format: ◯ 📕 ◯ 📱 ◯ 🎧

I've read the book:
In-full ◯   Partially ◯   Skimming ◯

Thoughts / Notes / Ideas

Book title:

Author:

Date started: | **Date finished:** | **No of pages:** | **My rating:**
☆☆☆☆☆

○ Fiction
Genre: ○ Non-fiction
Subject:

Format:

I've read the book:
In-full ○ Partially ○ Skimming ○

Thoughts / Notes / Ideas

Additional Notes / Comments / Takeaways / Quotes

Book title:

Author:

Date started:

Date finished:

No of pages:

My rating:
☆ ☆ ☆ ☆ ☆

○ Fiction
Genre:

○ Non-fiction
Subject:

Format:
○ ○ ○

I've read the book:
In-full   Partially   Skimming
○   ○   ○

Thoughts / Notes / Ideas

Additional Notes / Comments / Takeaways / Quotes

Book title:

Author:

Date started:

Date finished:

No of pages:

My rating:

☆ ☆ ☆ ☆ ☆

○ Fiction
Genre:

○ Non-fiction
Subject:

Format:

○ ◼ ○ ▤ ○ 🎧

I've read the book:

In-full
○

Partially
○

Skimming
○

Thoughts / Notes / Ideas

Additional Notes / Comments / Takeaways / Quotes

Book title:

Author:

Date started:	Date finished:	No of pages:	My rating:
			☆ ☆ ☆ ☆ ☆

◯ Fiction
Genre:

◯ Non-fiction
Subject:

Format:
◯ 📕 ◯ 📱 ◯ 🎧

I've read the book:
In-full ◯ Partially ◯ Skimming ◯

Thoughts / Notes / Ideas

Additional Notes / Comments / Takeaways / Quotes

Book title:

Author:

Date started:	Date finished:	No of pages:	My rating:
			☆ ☆ ☆ ☆ ☆

○ Fiction   ○ Non-fiction
Genre: Subject:

Format:
○ 📕 ○ 📱 ○ 🎧

I've read the book:
In-full   Partially   Skimming
○   ○   ○

Thoughts / Notes / Ideas

Additional Notes / Comments / Takeaways / Quotes

Book title:

Author:

Date started:

Date finished:

No of pages:

My rating:
☆ ☆ ☆ ☆ ☆

◯ Fiction
Genre:

◯ Non-fiction
Subject:

Format:
◯ 📕 ◯ 📱 ◯ 🎧

I've read the book:
In-full   Partially   Skimming
◯   ◯   ◯

Thoughts / Notes / Ideas

Additional Notes / Comments / Takeaways / Quotes

Book title:

Author:

Date started:

Date finished:

No of pages:

My rating:
☆ ☆ ☆ ☆ ☆

○ Fiction
Genre:

○ Non-fiction
Subject:

Format:
○ 📕 ○ 📱 ○ 🎧

I've read the book:
In-full   Partially   Skimming
○   ○   ○

Thoughts / Notes / Ideas

Additional Notes / Comments / Takeaways / Quotes

Book title:

Author:

Date started:

Date finished:

No of pages:

My rating:
☆ ☆ ☆ ☆ ☆

○ Fiction
Genre:

○ Non-fiction
Subject:

Format:
○ ▮ ○ 📄 ○ 🎧

I've read the book:
In-full   Partially   Skimming
○   ○   ○

Thoughts / Notes / Ideas

Additional Notes / Comments / Takeaways / Quotes

Book title:

Author:

Date started:	Date finished:	No of pages:	My rating:
			☆ ☆ ☆ ☆ ☆

○ Fiction   ○ Non-fiction
  Genre: Subject:

Format:
○ 📕 ○ 📱 ○ 🎧

I've read the book:
In-full   Partially   Skimming
  ○   ○   ○

Thoughts / Notes / Ideas

Additional Notes / Comments / Takeaways / Quotes

Book title:

Author:

Date started:

Date finished:

No of pages:

My rating:
☆ ☆ ☆ ☆ ☆

◯ Fiction
Genre:

◯ Non-fiction
Subject:

Format:

I've read the book:

In-full   Partially   Skimming
◯   ◯   ◯

Thoughts / Notes / Ideas

Additional Notes / Comments / Takeaways / Quotes

Book title:

Author:

Date started: | **Date finished:** | **No of pages:** | **My rating:**
☆☆☆☆☆

○ Fiction
Genre:

○ Non-fiction
Subject:

Format:
○ 📕 ○ 📱 ○ 🎧

I've read the book:
In-full | Partially | Skimming
○ | ○ | ○

Thoughts / Notes / Ideas

Additional Notes / Comments / Takeaways / Quotes

Book title:

Author:

Date started:	Date finished:	No of pages:	My rating:
			☆ ☆ ☆ ☆ ☆

○ Fiction
Genre:

○ Non-fiction
Subject:

Format:
○ 📕 ○ 📄 ○ 🎧

I've read the book:
In-full ○   Partially ○   Skimming ○

Thoughts / Notes / Ideas

Additional Notes / Comments / Takeaways / Quotes

Book title:

Author:

Date started:	Date finished:	No of pages:	My rating:
			☆ ☆ ☆ ☆ ☆

○ Fiction   ○ Non-fiction
  Genre: Subject:

Format:
○ 📕 ○ 📱 ○ 🎧

I've read the book:
In-full   Partially   Skimming
  ○   ○   ○

Thoughts / Notes / Ideas

Additional Notes / Comments / Takeaways / Quotes

Book title:

Author:

Date started:

Date finished:

No of pages:

My rating:
☆ ☆ ☆ ☆ ☆

◯ Fiction
Genre:

◯ Non-fiction
Subject:

Format:
◯ 📕 ◯ 📱 ◯ 🎧

I've read the book:
In-full   Partially   Skimming
◯   ◯   ◯

Thoughts / Notes / Ideas

Additional Notes / Comments / Takeaways / Quotes

Book title:

Author:

Date started:	Date finished:	No of pages:	My rating:
			☆ ☆ ☆ ☆ ☆

○ Fiction   ○ Non-fiction
Genre: Subject:

Format:
○ 📖   ○ 📱   ○ 🎧

I've read the book:
In-full   Partially   Skimming
○   ○   ○

Thoughts / Notes / Ideas

Additional Notes / Comments / Takeaways / Quotes

Book title:

Author:

Date started:

Date finished:

No of pages:

My rating:
☆ ☆ ☆ ☆ ☆

◯ Fiction
Genre:

◯ Non-fiction
Subject:

Format:

I've read the book:

In-full   Partially   Skimming
◯   ◯   ◯

Thoughts / Notes / Ideas

Additional Notes / Comments / Takeaways / Quotes

Book title:

Author:

Date started:

Date finished:

No of pages:

My rating:
☆ ☆ ☆ ☆ ☆

○ Fiction
Genre:

○ Non-fiction
Subject:

Format:
○ 📓 ○ 📱 ○ 🎧

I've read the book:
In-full ○   Partially ○   Skimming ○

Thoughts / Notes / Ideas

Additional Notes / Comments / Takeaways / Quotes

Book title:

Author:

Date started:

Date finished:

No of pages:

My rating:
☆ ☆ ☆ ☆ ☆

○ Fiction
Genre:

○ Non-fiction
Subject:

Format:
○ ○ ○

I've read the book:
In-full ○   Partially ○   Skimming ○

Thoughts / Notes / Ideas

Additional Notes / Comments / Takeaways / Quotes

Book title:

Author:

Date started:	Date finished:	No of pages:	My rating:
			☆ ☆ ☆ ☆ ☆

○ Fiction
Genre:

○ Non-fiction
Subject:

Format:
○ 📕 ○ 📱 ○ 🎧

I've read the book:
In-full	Partially	Skimming
○	○	○

Thoughts / Notes / Ideas

Additional Notes / Comments / Takeaways / Quotes

Book title:

Author:

Date started:	Date finished:	No of pages:	My rating:
			☆ ☆ ☆ ☆ ☆

◯ Fiction
   Genre:

◯ Non-fiction
   Subject:

Format:
◯ 📕   ◯ 📱   ◯ 🎧

I've read the book:
In-full   Partially   Skimming
◯   ◯   ◯

Thoughts / Notes / Ideas

Additional Notes / Comments / Takeaways / Quotes

Book title:

Author:

Date started:

Date finished:

No of pages:

My rating:
☆ ☆ ☆ ☆ ☆

◯ Fiction
Genre:

◯ Non-fiction
Subject:

Format:

I've read the book:

In-full ◯   Partially ◯   Skimming ◯

Thoughts / Notes / Ideas

Additional Notes / Comments / Takeaways / Quotes

Book title:

Author:

Date started:	Date finished:	No of pages:	My rating:
			☆ ☆ ☆ ☆ ☆

○ Fiction
Genre:

○ Non-fiction
Subject:

Format:
○ 📕 ○ 📱 ○ 🎧

I've read the book:
In-full ○   Partially ○   Skimming ○

Thoughts / Notes / Ideas

Additional Notes / Comments / Takeaways / Quotes

Book title:

Author:

Date started:

Date finished:

No of pages:

My rating:
☆ ☆ ☆ ☆ ☆

◯ Fiction
Genre:

◯ Non-fiction
Subject:

Format:

I've read the book:

In-full   Partially   Skimming
◯   ◯   ◯

Thoughts / Notes / Ideas

Additional Notes / Comments / Takeaways / Quotes

Book title:

Author:

Date started:	Date finished:	No of pages:	My rating: ☆ ☆ ☆ ☆ ☆

○ Fiction
Genre:

○ Non-fiction
Subject:

Format: ○ 📕 ○ 📱 ○ 🎧

I've read the book:
In-full ○   Partially ○   Skimming ○

Thoughts / Notes / Ideas

Additional Notes / Comments / Takeaways / Quotes

Book title:

Author:

Date started:	Date finished:	No of pages:	My rating: ☆☆☆☆☆

◯ Fiction
Genre:

◯ Non-fiction
Subject:

Format: ◯ ◯ ◯

I've read the book:
In-full   Partially   Skimming
◯   ◯   ◯

Thoughts / Notes / Ideas

Additional Notes / Comments / Takeaways / Quotes

Book title:

Author:

Date started:

Date finished:

No of pages:

My rating:
☆ ☆ ☆ ☆ ☆

○ Fiction
Genre:

○ Non-fiction
Subject:

Format:
○ 📕 ○ 📱 ○ 🎧

I've read the book:
In-full Partially Skimming
○   ○   ○

Thoughts / Notes / Ideas

Additional Notes / Comments / Takeaways / Quotes

Book title:

Author:

Date started:

Date finished:

No of pages:

My rating:
☆ ☆ ☆ ☆ ☆

○ Fiction
Genre:

○ Non-fiction
Subject:

Format:

I've read the book:

In-full   Partially   Skimming
  ○   ○   ○

Thoughts / Notes / Ideas

Additional Notes / Comments / Takeaways / Quotes

Books borrowed

Title / Author

From / Date / Return

Books lent out

Title / Author   To Whom / Date

Notes

Check out our **Author's Page** on **Amazon** for more interesting and useful logbooks, journals, agendas, planners and many other well-designed books.

Scan the QR code or search **Future Proof Publishing** on amazon.com

Thank you!

We hope you found our
Book Review Journal useful!

As a small family company, your
feedback is very important for us.

Any suggestions or recommendations
you might have are welcomed.

Please let us know how you like our
book at: **futureproofp@gmail.com**

Facebook:
@FutureProofP

Instagram:
@FutureProofP

Twitter:
@FutureProofP

Printed in Great Britain
by Amazon